How to Open a Store

A Step By Step Guide to Starting a Retail Shop Business

2019 Edition

MEIR LIRAZ

Published by BizMove
www.bizmove.com

Table of Contents

a. Excel Financial Projections Creator - simply type in your business' details and assumptions and it will automatically produce a comprehensive set of financial projections for your specific business, including: Start-Up Expenses, Projected Balance Sheet, Projected

Cash Flow Statement, Financial Ratios Analysis, Projected Profit and Loss Statement, Break Even Analysis, and more.

b. Detailed guide that will walk you step by step and show you exactly how to effectively use the above Excel Financial Projections Creator.

c. How to Improve Your Leadership and Management Skills (eBook) - Discover powerful strategies to motivate and inspire your people to bring out the best in them. Be the boss people want to give 200 percent for.

d. Small Business Management: Essential Ingredients for Success (eBook) - Learn effective business management tricks, secrets and shortcuts to make your business a success.

1. Basic Considerations and Requirements

This guide will walk you step by step through all the essential phases of starting a successful retail business. To profit in a retail business, you need to consider the following questions: What business am I in? What goods do I sell? Where is my market? Who will buy? Who is my competition? What is my sales strategy? What merchandising methods will I use? How much money is needed to operate my store? How will I get the work done? What management controls are needed? How can they be carried out? Where can I go for help?

As the owner, you have to answer these questions to draw up your business plan. The pages of this Guide are a combination of text and suggested analysis so that you can organize the information you gather from research to develop your plan, giving you a progression from a common sense starting point to a profitable ending point.

What Is a Business Plan?

The success of your business depends largely upon the decisions you make. A business plan allocates resources and measures the results of your actions, helping you set realistic goals and make logical decisions.

You may be thinking, "Why should I spend my time drawing up a business plan? What's in it for me?" If you've never worked out a plan, you are right in wanting to hear about the possible benefits before you do the work. Remember first that the lack of planning leaves you poorly equipped to anticipate future decisions and actions you must make or take to run your business successfully. A business plan Gives you a path to follow. A plan with goals and action steps allows you to guide your business through turbulent often unforeseen economic conditions.

A plan shows your banker the condition and direction of your business so that your business can be more favorably considered for a loan because of the banker's insight into your situation.

A plan can tell your sales personnel, suppliers, and others about your operations and goals.

A plan can help you develop as a manager. It can give you practice in thinking and figuring out problems about competitive conditions, promotional opportunities and situations that are good or bad for your business. Such practice over a period of time can help increase an owner-manager's ability to make judgments.

A second plan tells you what to do and how to do it to achieve the goals you have set for your business.

What Business Am I In?

In making your business plan, the first question to consider is: What business am I really in? At first reading, this question may seem silly. "If there is one thing I know," you say to yourself, "it is what business I'm in." Hold on and think. Some owner-managers have gone broke and others have wasted their savings because they did not define their businesses in detail. Actually they were confused about what business they were in.

Look at an example. Mr. Jet maintained a dock and sold and rented boats. He thought he was in the marina business. But when he got into trouble and asked for outside help, he learned that he was not necessarily in the marina business. He was in several businesses. He was in the restaurant business with a dockside cafe, serving meals to boating parties. He was in the real estate business, buying and selling lots. He was in boat repair business, buying parts and hiring a mechanic as demand rose. Mr. Jet was trying to be too many things and couldn't decide which venture to put money into and how much return to expect. What slim resources he had were fragmented.

Before he could make a profit on his sales and a return on his investment, Mr. Jet had to decide what business he really was in and concentrate on it. After much study, he realized that he should stick to the marina format, buying, selling, and servicing boats.

Decide what business you are in and write it down - define your business.
To help you decide, think of answers to questions like: What do you buy? What do you sell? Which of your lines of goods yields the greatest profit? What do people ask you for? What is it that you are trying to do better or more of or differently from your competitors? Write it down in detail.

2. Planning Your Marketing

When you have decided what business you are in, you are ready to consider another important part of you business plan. Marketing. Successful marketing starts with the owner-manager. You have to know the merchandise you sell and the wishes and wants of your customers you can appeal to. The objective is to move the stock off the shelves and display racks at the right price and bring in sales dollars.

The text and suggested working papers that follow are designed to help you work out a marketing plan for your store.

Determining the Sales Potential

In retail business, your sales potential depends on location. Like a tree, a store has to draw its nourishment from the area around it. The following questions should help you work through the problem of selecting a profitable location.

In what part of the city or town will you locate?

In the downtown business section?

In the area right next to the downtown business area?

In a residential section of the town?

On the highway outside of town?

In the suburbs?

In a suburban shopping center?

On a worksheet, write where you plan to locate and give your reasons why you chose that particular location.

Now consider these questions that will help you narrow down a place in your location area.

What is the competition in the area you have picked?

How many of the stores look prosperous?

How many look as though they are barely getting by?

How many similar stores went out of business in this area last year?

How many new stores opened up in the last year?

What price line does competition carry?

Which store or stores in the area will be your biggest competitors?

Again, write down the reasons for your opinions. Also write out an analysis of the area's economic base and give the reason for your opinion. Is the area in which you plan to locate supported by a strong economic base? For example, are nearby industries working full time? Only part time? Did any industries go out of business in the past several months?

Are new industries scheduled to open in the next several months?

When you find a store building that seems to be what you need, answer the following questions:

Is the neighborhood starting to get run down?

Is the neighborhood new and on the way up? (The local Chamber of Commerce may have census data for your area. Census Tracts on Population, published by the Bureau of Census, may be useful. Other sources on such marketing statistics are trade associations and directories).

Are there any super highways or through-ways planned for the neighborhood?

Is street traffic fairly heavy all day?

How close is the building to bus lines and other transportation?

Are there adequate parking spaces convenient to your store?

Are the sidewalks in good repair (you may have to repair them)?

is the street lighting good?

Is your store on the sunny side of the street?

What is the occupancy history of this store building? Does the store have a reputation for failures? (Have stores opened and closed after a short time)?

Why have other businesses failed in this location?

What is the physical condition of the store?

What service does the landlord provide?

What are the terms of the lease?

How much rent must you pay each month?

Estimate the gross annual sales you expect in this location.

When you think you have finally solved the site location question, ask your banker to recommend people who know most about location in your line of business. Contact these people and listen to their advice and opinions, weigh what they say, then decide.

3. How to Attract Customers

When you have a location in mind, you should work through another aspect of marketing. How will you attract customers to your store? How will you pull business away from your competition?

It is in working with this aspect of marketing that many retailers find competitive advantages. The ideas that they develop are as good as and often better than those that large companies develop. The work blocks that follow are designed to help you think about image, pricing, customer service policies, and advertising.

Image

A store has an image whether or not the owner is aware of it. For example, throw some merchandise onto shelves and onto display tables in a dirty, dimly lit store and you've got an image. Shoppers think of it as a dirty, junky store and avoid coming into it. Your image should be concrete enough to promote in your advertising and other promotional activities. For example, "home-cooked" food might be the image of a small restaurant.

Write out on a worksheet the image that you want shoppers and customers to have of your store.

Pricing

Value received is the key to pricing. The only way a store can have low prices is to sell low-priced merchandise. Thus, what you do about the prices you charge depends on the lines of merchandise you buy and sell. It depends also on what your competition charges for these lines of merchandise. Your answers to the following questions should help you to decide what to do about pricing.

In what price ranges are your line of merchandise sold

High _____ , Medium _____, or Low _____?

Will you sell for cash only?

What services will you offer to justify your prices if they are higher than your competitor's prices?

If you offer credit, will your price have to be higher than if all sales are for cash? The credit costs have to come from somewhere. Plan for them.

If you use credit card systems, what will it cost you? Will you have to add to your prices to absorb this cost.

Customer Service Policies

The service you provide your customers may be free to them, but you pay for it. For example, if you provide free parking, you pay for your own parking lot or pick up your part of the cost of a lot you share with other retailers.

Make a list of the services that your competitors offer and estimate the cost of each service. How many of these services will you have to provide just to be competitive? Are there other services that would attract customers but that competitors are not offering? If so, what are your estimates of the cost of such services? Now list all the services you plan to offer and the estimated costs. Total this expense and figure out how you can include those added costs in your prices without pricing your merchandise out of the market.

4. Planning Your Advertising Activities

Advertising was saved until the last because you have to have something to say before advertising can be effective. When you have an image, price range, and customer services, you are ready to tell prospective customers why they should shop in your store.

When the money you can spend for advertising is limited, it is vital that your advertising be on target. Before you think about how much money you can afford for advertising, take time to determine what jobs you want to do for your store. List what makes your store different from your competitors. List the facts about your store and its merchandise that your advertising should tell shoppers and prospective customers.

When you have these facts listed and in hand, you are ready to think about the form your advertising should take and its cost. Ask the local media (newspapers, radio and television, and printers of direct mail pieces) for information about the services and results they offer for your money.

How you spend advertising money is your decision, but don't fall into the trap that snares many advertisers who have little or no experience with advertising copy and media selection. Advertising is a profession. Don't spend a lot of money on advertising without getting professional advice on what kind and how much advertising your store needs.

The following work sheet can be useful in determining what advertising is needed to sell your strong points to prospective customers.

Form of Advertising	Size of Audience	Frequency of Use	Cost of a single ad	Est. Cost
_____	_____	_____	_____	_____
_____	_____	_____	_____	_____
_____	_____	_____	_____	_____
_____	_____	_____	_____	_____
			Total	_____

When you have a figure on what your advertising for the next twelve months will cost, check it against what similar stores spend. Advertising expense is one of the operating ratios (expenses as a percentage of sales) that trade associations and other organizations gather. If your estimated cost for advertising is substantially higher than this average for your line of merchandise, take a second look. No single expense item should be allowed to get way out of line if you want to make a profit. Your task in determining how much to spend for advertising comes down to the question, "How much can I afford to spend and still do the job that needs to be done?"

In-store Sales Promotion

To complete your work on marketing, you need to think about what you want to happen after prospects get inside your store. Your goal is to move stock off your shelves and displays at a profit and satisfy your customers. You want repeat customers and money in your cash register.

At this point, if you have decided to sell for cash only, take a second look at your decision. Don't overlook the fact that Americans like to buy on credit. Often a credit card, or other system of credit and collections, is needed to attract and hold customers. Customers will have more buying confidence and be more comfortable in your store if they know they can afford to buy. Credit makes this possible.

To encourage people to buy, self-service stores rely on layout, attractive displays, signs and clearly marked prices on the items offered for sale. Other stores combine these techniques with personal selling.

List the display counters, racks, special equipment (something peculiar to your business like a frozen food display bin or a machine to measure and cut cloth), and other fixtures. Figure the cost of all fixtures and equipment by listing them on a worksheet as follows:

Type of equipment	Number	X Unit Cost	= Cost
_____	_____	_____	_____
_____	_____	_____	_____
_____	_____	_____	_____
_____	_____	_____	_____
_____	_____	_____	_____

Draw several layouts of your store and attach the layout that suits you to the cost worksheet. Determine how many signs you may need for a twelve month operation and estimate that cost also.

If your store is a combination of self-service and personal selling, how many sales persons and cashiers will you need? Estimate, I will need _____ sales persons at $ _____ each week (include payroll taxes and insurance in this salaries cost). In a year, salaries will cost: _____.

Personal attention to customers is one strong point that a store can use as a competitive tool. You want to emphasize in training employees that everyone has to pitch in and get the job done. Customers are not interested in job descriptions, but they are interested in being served promptly and courteously. Nothing is more frustrating to a customer than being ignored by an employee. Decide what training you will give your sales people in the techniques of how to greet customers, show merchandise, suggest other items, and handle customer needs and complaints.

Buying

When buying merchandise for resale, you need to answer questions such as:

Who sells the line to retailers? Is it sold by the manufacturer directly or through wholesalers and distributors?

What delivery service can you get and must you pay shipping charges?

What are the terms of buying?

Can you get credit?

How quickly can the vendor deliver fill-in orders?

You should establish a source of supply on acceptable terms for each line of merchandise and estimate a plan for purchasing as follows:

Name of Item	Name of Supplier	Address Supplier	Disc. Offered	Delv. Time(1)	Freight Costs(2)	Fill-in Policy(3)
___	___	___	___	___	___	___
___	___	___	___	___	___	___
___	___	___	___	___	___	___

(1) How many days or weeks does it take the supplier to deliver the merchandise to your store.

(2) Who pays? You, the buyer? The supplier? Freight or transportation costs are a big expense item.

(3) What is the supplier's policy on fill-in orders? That is, do you have to buy a gross, a dozen, or will the supplier ship only two or

three items? How long does it take for the delivery to get into your store?

Stock Control

Often shoppers leave without buying because the store did not have the items they wanted or the sizes and colors were wrong. Stock control, combined with suppliers whose policies on fill-in orders are favorable to you, provides a way to reduce "walkouts".

The type of system you use to keep informed about your stock, or inventory, depends on your line of merchandise and the delivery dates provided by your suppliers.

Your stock control system should enable you to determine what needs to be ordered on the basis of: (1) what is on hand, (2) what is on order, and (3) what has been sold. Some trade associations and suppliers provide systems to members and customers, otherwise your accountant can set up a system that is best for your business. Inventory control is based upon either a perpetual or a periodic method of accounting that involves cost considerations as well as stock control. When you have decided what system you will use to control stock, estimate its cost. You may not need an extensive (and expensive) control system because you do not need the detailed information such a system collects. The system must justify its costs or you will just waste money and time on a useless effort.

Stock Turnover

When an owner-manager buys reasonably well, you can expect to turnover stock several times a year. For example, the stock in a small camera shop should turnover four times to four and a half times a year. What is the average stock turnover per year of your line of merchandise? How many times do you expect your stock to turnover? List the reasons for your estimate.

Behind-the-Scenes Work

In a retail store, behind-the-scenes work consists of the receiving of merchandise, preparing it for display, maintaining display counters and shelves, and keeping the store clean and attractive to customers. The following analytical list will help you decided what to do and the cost of those actions.

First list the equipment (for example a marking machine for pricing, shelves, a cash register) you will need for: (1) receiving merchandise (2) preparing merchandise for display, (3) maintaining display counters and shelves, and (4) keeping the store clean. Next list the supplies you will need for a year, for example, brooms, price tags, and business forms.

Use this format to figure these costs:

Name of Equip./Supplies	Quantity	X Unit Cost	= Cost
_____	_____	_____	_____
_____	_____	_____	_____
_____	_____	_____	_____

Who will do the back-room work and the cleaning that is needed to make a smooth operation in the store? If you do it yourself, how many hours a week will it take you? Will you do these chores after closing? If you use employees, what will they cost? On a worksheet describe how you plan to handle these tasks. For example:

Back-room work will be done by one employee during the slack sales times of the day. I estimate that the employee will spend _____ hours per week on these tasks and will cost _____ (number of hours times hourly wages) per week and _____ per year.

I will need _____ square feet of space for the back-room operation. This space will cost _____ per square foot or a total of _____ per month.

List and analyze all expense items in the same manner. Examples are utilities, office help, insurance, telephone, postage, accountant, payroll taxes, and licenses or other local taxes. If you plan to hire others to help manage, analyze these salaries.

5. How Much Money Will You Need

At this point, take some time to think about what your business plan means in terms of dollars. This section is designed to help you put your plan into dollars.

The first question concerns the source of dollars. After your initial capital investments in a retail store, the main source of money is sales. What sales volume do you expect to do in the first twelve months? Write your estimate here _____, and justify your estimate.

Start-Up Costs:

List the following estimated start-up costs:

Fixtures and equipment*	_____
Starting inventory	_____
Decorating and remodeling	_____
Installation of equipment	_____
Deposits for utilities	_____
Legal and professional fees	_____
Licenses and permits	_____
Advertising for the opening	_____
Accounts receivable	_____
Operating cash	_____
Total	_____

*Transfer your figures from previous worksheets.

Whether you have the funds (say in savings) or borrow the money, your new business will have to pay back start-up costs. Keep this fact in mind as you work on estimating expenses and on other financial aspects of your plan.

Expenses

In connection with annual sales volume you need to think about expenses. If, for example, you plan to do sales amounting to $100,000, what will it cost you to do this amount of business? How much profit will you make? A business must make a profit or close.

The following exercise will help you to make an estimate of your expenses. To do this exercise you need to know the total cost of goods sold for your line of merchandise for the period (month or year) that you are analyzing. Cost of goods sold is expressed as a percentage of sales and is called an operating ratio. Check with your trade association to get the operating ratios for your business's. The following is the format for an Income Statement with operating ratios substituted for dollar amounts.

Summary of Operating Ratios
of 250 high Profit Hardware Stores

	Percent of sale
Sales	100.00
Cost of Goods Sold	-64.92
Margin	35.08
Expenses	
Payroll and other employee expenses	16.23
Occupancy expenses	3.23
Office supplies and postage	0.40
Advertising	1.49
donations	0.08
Telephone and telegraph	0.24
Bad Debts	0.30
Delivery	0.47
Insurance	0.66
Taxes (other than realestate and payroll)	0.46
Interest	0.61
Depreciation (other than real estate)	0.57
Supplies	0.37
Legal and accounting expenses	0.31
Dues and subscription	0.08
Travel, buying, and entertainment	0.19
Unclassified expenses	0.64
Total operating expense	-26.33
Net operating profit	8.75
Other income	1.65
Net profit before income taxes	10.40

Now using your operating ratio for cost of goods sold and your estimated Sales Revenue, you can breakdown your expenses by substituting your ratios and dollar amounts in the Income Statement.

Notice that Gross Margin must be large enough to provide for your expenses and profit.

	Expressed in Percent	Expressed in dollars	Your Percentage	Your Dollars
1. Sales	100	$100,000	100	$___
2. Cost of Goods Sold	-66	-66,000	___	-$___
3. Gross Margin	34	$34,000	___	$___

and continue to fill out the entire Income Statement. Work out statements monthly or for the year.

Cash Forecast

A budget helps you to see the dollar amount of your expected revenue and expenses each month. Then from month to month the question is: Will sales bring in enough money to pay for the store's bills? The owner-manager must prepare for the financial peaks and valleys of the business cycle. A cash forecast is a management tool that can eliminate much of the anxiety that can plague you if your sales go through lean months. Use the following format.

Estimated Cash Forecast

	Jan	Feb	Mar	Apr	May	Jun	Jul	Aug	Sep	Oct	Nov	Dec	Total
(1) Cash in Bank (Start of Month)	—	—	—	—	—	—	—	—	—	—	—	—	—
(2) Petty Cash (Start of Month)	—	—	—	—	—	—	—	—	—	—	—	—	—
(3) Total Cash (add (1) and (2))	—	—	—	—	—	—	—	—	—	—	—	—	—
(4) Expected Accounts Receivable	—	—	—	—	—	—	—	—	—	—	—	—	—
(5) Other Money Expected	—	—	—	—	—	—	—	—	—	—	—	—	—
(6) Total Receipts (add (4) and (5))	—	—	—	—	—	—	—	—	—	—	—	—	—
(7) Total Cash and Receipts (add (3) and (6))	—	—	—	—	—	—	—	—	—	—	—	—	—
(8) All Disbursements (for month)	—	—	—	—	—	—	—	—	—	—	—	—	—
(9) Cash Balance at end of Month in Bank Account and Petty Cash (subtract (8) from (7)*	—	—	—	—	—	—	—	—	—	—	—	—	—

*This balance is your starting figure for the next month

Is Additional Money Needed? Suppose at this point that your business needs more money than can be generated by present sales. What do you do? If your business has great potential or is in good financial condition, as shown by its balance sheet, you will borrow money (from a bank most likely) to keep the business operating during start-up and slow sales periods. The loan can be repaid during the fat sales months when sales are greater than expenses. Adequate working capital is needed for success and survival; but cash on hand (or the lack of it) is not necessarily an indication that the business is in bad financial shape. A lender will look at your balance sheet to see the business's Net Worth of which cash and cash flow are only a part. The balance sheet statement shows a business's Net Worth (financial position) at a given point in time, say at the close of business at the end of the month or at the end of the year. Free Retail Business Plan How To.

Even if you do not need to borrow money you may want to show your plan and balance sheet to your banker. It is never too early to build good relations and credibility (trust) with your banker. Let your banker know that you are a manager who knows where you want to go rather than someone who merely hopes to succeed.

Control and Feedback

To make your plan work you need feedback. For example, the year-end profit and loss (income) statement shows whether your business made a profit or took a loss for the past twelve months.

Don't wait twelve months for the score. To keep your plan on target you need readings at frequent intervals. An income statement compiled at the end of each month or at the end of each quarter is one type of frequent feedback. Also you must set up management controls that help you insure that the right things are done each day and week. Organization is needed because you as the owner-manager cannot do all the work. You must delegate work, responsibility, and authority. The record keeping systems should be set up before the store opens. After you're in business it is too late.

The control system that you set up should give you information about stock, sales, receipts and disbursement. The simpler the accounting control system, the better. Its purpose is to give you current useful information. You need facts that expose trouble spots. Outside advisers, such as accountants can help.

Stock Control

The purpose of controlling stock is to provide maximum service to your customers. Your aim should be to achieve a high turnover rate on your inventory. The fewer dollars you tie up in stock, the better.

In a store, stock control helps the owner-manager offer customers a balanced assortment and enables you to determine what needs ordering on the basis of (1) what is on hand, (2) what is on order, and (3) what has been sold.

When setting up inventory controls, keep in mind that the cost of the stock is not your only cost. There are inventory costs, such as the cost of purchasing, the cost of keeping stock control records, and the cost of receiving and storing stock.

Sales

In a store, sales slips and cash register tapes give the owner-manager feedback at the end of each day. To keep on top of sales, you need answers to questions, such as: How many sales were made? What was the dollar amount? What were the best selling products? At what price? What credit terms were given to customers?

Receipts

Break out your receipts into receivables (money still owned such as a charge sale) and cash. You know how much credit you have given, how much more you can give, and how much cash you have with which to operate.

Disbursement

Your management controls should also give you information about the dollars your company pays out. In checking on your bills, you do not want to be penny-wise and pound-foolish. You should pay bills on time to take advantage of supplier discounts. Your review systems should also give you the opportunity to make judgments on the use of the funds. In this manner, you can be on top of emergencies as well as routine situations. Your system should also keep you aware that tax monies, such as payroll income tax deductions, must be set aside and paid out at the proper time.

6. Break-Even Analysis

Break-even analysis is a management control device that approximates how much you must sell in order to cover your costs with no profit and no loss. Profit comes after break-even.

Profit depends on sales volume, selling price, and costs. Break-even analysis helps you to estimate what a change in one or more of these factories will do to your profit. To figure a break-even point, fixed costs (like rent) must be separated from variable costs (like the cost of goods sold).

The break-even formula is:

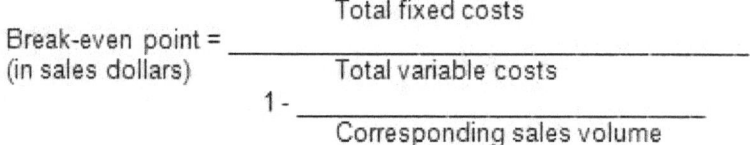

$$\text{Break-even point} = \frac{\text{Total fixed costs}}{1 - \dfrac{\text{Total variable costs}}{\text{Corresponding sales volume}}}$$

(in sales dollars)

Sample break-even calculations: Bill Mason plans to open a shoe store and estimates his fixed expenses at about $9,000 the first year. He estimates variable expenses of about $700 for every $1,000 of sales. How much must the store gross to break-even?

$$\text{BE point} = \cfrac{\$9{,}000}{1 - \cfrac{700}{1{,}000}} = \frac{\$9{,}000}{1 - 0.70} = \frac{\$9{,}000}{30} = \$30{,}000$$

Is Your Plan Workable?

Stop when you have worked out your break-even point. Whether the break-even point looks realistic or way off base, it is time to make sure that your plan is workable.

Take time to re-examine your plan before you back it with money. If the plan is not workable, better to learn it now than to realize six months down the road that you are pouring money into a losing venture.

In reviewing your plan, look at the cost figures you drew up when you broke down your expenses for the year (operating ratios on the income statement). If any of your cost items are too high or too low, change them. You can write your changes above or below your original entries on the worksheet. When you finish making your adjustments, you will have a revised projected statement of sales and expenses.

With your revised figures, work out a revised break-even analysis. Whether the new break-even point looks good or bad, take one more precaution. Show your plan to someone who has not been involved in working out the details with you. Get an impartial. knowledgeable second opinion. Your banker, or other advisor may see weaknesses that failed to appear as you went over the plan details. These experts may see strong points that your plan should emphasize.

Put Your Plan Into Action

When your plan is as thorough and accurate as possible you are ready to put it into action. Keep in mind that action is the difference between a plan and a dream. If a plan is not acted upon, it is of no more value than a wishful dream. A successful owner-manager does not stop after gathering information and drawing up a business plan, as you have done in working through this Guide. use the plan.

At this point, look back over your plan. Look for things that must be done to put your plan into action. What needs to be done will depend on your situation and goals. For example, if your business plan calls for an increase in sales, you may have to provide more funds for this expansion. Have you more money to put into this business? Do you borrow from friends and relatives? From your bank? From your suppliers (through credit terms?) If you are starting a new business, one action may be to get a loan for fixtures, stock, employee salaries, and other expenses. Another action will be to find and to hire capable employees.

Now make a list of things that must be done to put your plan into action. Give each item a date so that it can be done at the appropriate time.

To put my plan into action, I must:

1. Do (action) _____ By _____(date)

2. etc.

Keep Your Plan Current

Once you put your plan into action, look out for changes. They can cripple the best business no matter how well planned. Stay on top of changing conditions and adjust your business plan accordingly. Sometimes the change is within your company. For example, several of your sales persons may quit. Sometimes the change is with the customers whose desires and tastes shift and change or refuse to change. Sometimes the change is technological as when products are created and marketed.

In order to adjust your plan to account for such changes, you the owner-manager, must:

Be alert to the changes that come about in your line of business, in your market, and in your customers.

Check your plan against these changes.

Determine what revisions, if any, are needed in the business plan.

The method you use to keep your plan current so that your business can weather the changing forces of the market place is up to you. Read trade and business papers and magazines and review your plan periodically. Once each month or every other month, go over your plan to see whether or not it needs adjusting. Certainly you will have more accurate dollar amounts to work with after you have been in business for a time. Make revisions and put them into action. You must be constantly updating and improving. A good business plan must evolve from experience and the best current information. A good business plan is good business.

7. How to Find the Best Location for Your Store

A retail consultant was asked, "What are the three factors most likely to ensure retailing success?" The reply was, "(1) Retail Locations, (2) Retail Locations, and (3) Retail location."

In other words, the impact of retail store locations and choosing retail location on the success of your store operation can't be overstressed! This guide is aimed at just one aspect of how to determine the proper site, namely, research into the traffic in that area - both vehicular and pedestrian - that will bring business into your store. Methods of taking a traffic count are discussed along with how to evaluate and interpret the collected data.

Importance of a Good Retail Location

Often an owner-manager, for whatever reason, is faced with renewing the lease or choosing a new or perhaps an additional site for business. At this crucial time the owner should consider the value of a traffic count to be sure the new location can draw customers into the store.

In the central business district, land values and rents are often based on traffic counts. The site in the central business district that produces the highest traffic count with regard to the type of traffic desired by a particular store is considered its 100 percent location. However, a 100 percent location for one type of store may not be 100 percent for other types. For example, a site which rates 100 percent for a drugstore may be only 80 percent for a men's clothing shop or 60 percent for an appliance store.

In recent years, for most lines of trade, the average store size has increased. This, of course, means greater financial outlay for a good location plus greater investment in inventory, fixtures, and personnel. Did you know that firms which conduct location research generally eliminate about four out of every five locations studied?

Factors to be Considered in Choosing Retail Locations

Three factors confront you as an owner-manager in choosing a location: selection of a city; choice of an area or type of location within a city; and identification of a specific site.

If you are going to relocate in another city, naturally you consider the following factors:

Size of the city's trading area.

Population and population trends in the trading area.

Total purchasing power and the distribution of the purchasing power.

Total retail trade potential for different lines of trade.

Number, size, and quality of competition.

Progressiveness of competition.

In choosing an area or type of location within a city you evaluate factors such as:

Customer attraction power of the particular store and the shopping district.

Quantitative and qualitative nature of competitive stores.

Availability of access routes to the stores.

Nature of zoning regulations.

Direction of the area expansion.

General appearance of the area.

Pinpointing the specific site is particularly important. In central and secondary business districts, small stores depend upon the traffic created by large stores. Large stores in turn depend on attracting customers from the existing flow of traffic. (However, where sales depend on nearby residents, selecting the trading area is more important than picking the specific site.) Obviously, you want to know about the following factors when choosing a specific site:

Adequacy and potential passing the site.

Ability of the site to intercept traffic en route from one place to another.

Complementary nature of the adjacent stores.

Adequacy of parking.

Vulnerability of the site to unfriendly competition.

Cost of the site.

How to Make a Traffic Count

First of all, be sure you need a traffic count. Although knowledge of the volume and character of passing traffic is always useful, in certain cases a traffic survey may not really make an difference. Other selection factors involved may be so significant that the outcome of a traffic study will have relatively little bearing on your decision. When the other selection factors, such as parking, operating costs, or location of competitors, become less important and data on traffic flow becomes dominant, then a counts is indicated. Once you have determined that you really need a traffic count, the general objective is to count the passing traffic - both pedestrian and vehicular - that would constitute potential customers who would probably be attracted into your type of store. To evaluate the traffic available to competitors, you may desire to conduct traffic counts at their sites, too.

Data from a traffic count should not only show how many people pass by but generally indicate what kinds of people they are. Analysis of the characteristics of the passing traffic often reveals patterns and variations not readily apparent from casual observation.

For counting purposes, the passing traffic is divided into different classifications according to the characteristics of the customers who would patronize your type of business. Whereas a drugstore is interested in the total volume of passing traffic, a men's clothing store is obviously more concerned with the amount of male traffic, especially men between the ages of sixteen and sixty-five.

It is also important to classify passing traffic by its reasons for passing. A woman on the way to a beauty salon is probably poor prospect for a drugstore. The hours at which individuals go by are often an indication of their purpose. In the early morning hours people are generally on their way to work. In the late afternoon these same people are usually going home from work. When one chain organization estimates the number of potential women customers passing a site between 10 a.m and 5 p.m. to be the serious shoppers.

Evaluation of the financial bracket of passersby is also significant. Out of 100 women passing a prospective location for an exclusive dress shop, only ten may appear to have the income to patronize the shop. Of course, the greater your experience in a particular retail trade, the more accurately you can estimate the number of your potential customers. To determine what proportion of the passing traffic represents your potential shoppers, some of the pedestrians should be interviewed about the origin of their trip, their destination, and the stores in which they plan to shop. This sort of information can provide you with a better estimate of the number of potential customers.

In summary, the qualitative information gathered about the passing traffic should include counting the individuals who seem to possess the characteristics appropriate to the desired clientele, judging their reasons for using that route, and calculating their ability to buy.

Pedestrian Traffic Count

In making a pedestrian count you must decide: who is to be counted; where the count should take place; and when the count should be made. In considering who is to be counted, determine what types of people should be included. For example, the study might count all men presumed to be between sixteen and sixty-five. The directions should be completely clear as to the individuals to be counted so the counters will be consistent and the total figure will reflect the traffic flow.

As previously indicated, it is frequently desirable to divide the pedestrian traffic into classes. Quite often separate counts of men and women and certain age categories are wanted. A trial run will indicate if there are any difficulties in identifying those to be counted or in placing them into various groupings.

You next determine the specific place where the count is to be taken. You decide whether all the traffic near the site should be counted or only the traffic passing directly in front of the site. Remember that if all the pedestrians passing through an area are counted, there is the possibility of double counting. Since a person must both enter and leave an area, it is important that each person be counted only once - either when entering or when leaving. Therefore, it is essential that the counter consistently counts at the same location.

When the count should be taken is influenced by the season, month, week, day, and hour. For example, during the summer season there is generally an increased flow of traffic on the shady side of the street. During a holiday period such as the month before Christmas or the week before Easter, traffic is denser than it is regularly. The patronage of a store varies by day of the week, too. Store traffic usually increased during the latter part of a week. In some communities, on factory paydays and days when social security checks are received, certain locations experience heavier than normal traffic.

The day of the week and the time of day should represent a normal period for traffic flow. Pedestrian flow accelerates around noon as office workers go out for lunch. Generally more customers enter a downtown store between 10 a.m. and noon and between 1 p.m. and 3 p.m. than at any other time. Local custom or other factors, however, may cause a variation in these expected traffic patterns.

After you choose the day that has normal traffic flow, the day should be divided into half-hour and hourly intervals. Traffic should be counted and recorded for each half-hour period of a store's customary operating hours. If it is not feasible to count the traffic for each half-hour interval, the traffic flow can be sampled. Traffic in representative half-hours periods in the morning, noon, afternoon, and evening can be counted.

Estimate of Store Sales

Data from a pedestrian traffic survey can give you information on whether or not the site would generate a profitable volume for your store. A retailer with some past experience in the same merchandise line for which a store is planned can make a reasonable estimate of sales volume if the following information is available (in lieu of past personal experience, the trade association for your type of business may be of help):

Characteristics of individuals who are most likely to be store customers (from pedestrian interviews).

Number of such individuals passing the site during store hours (from traffic counts).

Proportion of passersby who will enter the store (from pedestrian interviews).

Proportion of those entering who will become purchasers (from pedestrian interviews).

Amount of the average transaction (from past experience, trade associations, and trade publication).

One retailer divides the people who pass a given site into three categories: those who enter a store; those who after looking at the windows, may become customers; and those who pass without entering or looking. Owing to prior experience, this retailer is able to estimate from the percentage falling into each classification not only the number who will make purchases but also how much the average purchase will be. If, out of 1,000 passerbys each day, five percent enter (fifty) and each spends an average of $8 ($400), a store at that site which operates 300 days a year will have an annual sales volume of $120,000.

Types of Consumer Goods

Another factor that affects site selection is the customers' view of the goods sold by a store.

Consumers tend to group products into three major categories: convenience, shopping, and specialty.

Convenience usually means low unit price, purchased frequently, little selling effort, bought by habit, and sold in numerous outlets. Examples: candy bars, cigarettes, and milk.

Shopping usually means high unit price, purchased infrequently, more intensive selling effort usually required on the part of the store owner, price and features compared, and sold in selectively franchised outlets. Examples: men's suits, automobiles, and furniture.

Specialty usually means high unit price although price is not a purchase consideration, bought infrequently, requires a special effort on the part of the customer to make the purchase, no substitutes considered, and sold in exclusively franchised outlets. Examples: precious jewelry, expensive perfumes, fine furs, and so on, of specific brands or name labels.

For store handling convenience goods, the quantity of pedestrian traffic is most important, The corner of an intersection which offers two distinct traffic streams and a large window display area is usually a better site that the middle of a block. Downtown convenience goods stores, such as low-priced, ready-to-wear stores and drugstores, have a limited ability to generate their own traffic, Therefore they must be situated in or near their 100 percent block. In merchandising convenience goods, it is easier to build the store within the traffic than the traffic within the store. Convenience goods are often purchased on impulse in easily accessible stores.

For stores handling shopping goods, the quality of the traffic is more important. While convenience goods are purchased by nearly everyone, certain kinds of shopping goods are purchased by only certain segments of shoppers. Moreover, it is sometimes the character of the retail establishment rather than its type of goods that governs the selection of a site. For example, a conventional men's wear store should be in a downtown location close to a traffic generator like a department store. On the other hand, a discount store handling menswear would prefer an accessible highway location, Stores that generate their own traffic through extensive promotional effort can locate away from the 100 percent location.

In many cases, buyers of shopping goods like to compare the items in several stores by traveling only a minimum distance. As a result stores offering complementary items tend to locate close to one another. An excellent site for a shopping goods store is next to a department store or between two large department stores where traffic flows between them. Another good site is one between a major parking area and a department store.

Specialty goods are often sought by consumers who are already "sold" on the product, brand, or both. Stores catering to this type of consumer may use isolated locations because they generate their own consumer traffic.

Stores carrying specialty goods that are complementary to certain other kinds of shopping goods may desire to locate close to the shopping goods stores. In general, the specialty goods retailer should locate in the type of neighborhood where the adjacent stores and other establishments are compatible with his or her operation.

Automobile Traffic Count

A growing number of retail firms depend on drive-in traffic for their sales. Both the quantity and quality of automotive traffic can be analyzed in the same way as pedestrian traffic. For the major streets in urban areas, either the city engineer, the planning commission, the State highway department, or an outdoor advertising company may be able to provide you with data on traffic flows. However, you may need to modify this information to suit your special needs. For example, you should supplement data relating to total count of vehicles passing the site with actual observation in order to evaluate such influences on traffic as commercial vehicles, changing of shifts at nearby factories, through highway traffic, and increased flow caused by special events or activities. Retail locations.

Type of Trips

Automobile traffic may be classified according to the reason for the trip. There are the work trip, the shopping trip, and the pleasure trip. Knowledge of the type of trip can assist you in making the correct site decision, Careful observation of the character of the traffic and even a few short interviews with drivers who are stopped for a traffic signal will reveal the nature of their trips.

Different types of retailers seek different locations although they are serving the same type of customer. For example, to serve a work trip customer, a dry-cleaner and a convenience foodstore usually desire to be located on different sides of the street. The dry-cleaner wants to locate on the going-to-work side of the street while the convenience foodstore wants to be on the going-home side.

A good location for a retailer seeking the customer on a planned shopping trip is along the right-hand side of the main street leading into a shopping district and adjacent to other streets carrying traffic into, out of, or across town. The beginning or end of a row of stores rather than across the street from the stores is preferable, Noting on which side the older, established stores are located provides a clue to the best side of the street. But check it out to be sure that the sales in these stores are rising rather than declining.

In smaller communities, where the major streets lead to and from the downtown area, the traffic pattern can be readily identified. In larger cities, where there are suburban shopping center location, the traffic moves in many different directions. Because shopping centers tend to generate traffic, an analysis of the traffic flow to centers and between centers may show that a particular store location is outstanding.

The person on a pleasure of recreational trip is in the market for services such as those offered by motels, restaurants, and service stations. The probability of attracting this type of customer increases if the facility is located alongside a well-traveled highway and adjacent to a major entrance to the community.

Types of Consumer Goods

Understanding the motives of people passing your site in cars also depends on the same analysis of consumer behavior used in classifying pedestrians. There are the same three categories of goods or products to consider: convenience, shopping and specialty.

In general, the greater the automobile traffic, the greater the sales of convenience goods for catering to the drive-in traffic. For the drive-in store selling low-priced convenience goods, the volume of traffic passing the site is a most important factor in making a site decision. The consumer purchases these goods frequently and desires them to be readily available. Consumers are reminded when passing a convenience goods store that he or she needs a particular item.

If the consumer must make a special trip to purchase such convenience staple goods as food and drug items, they want the store to be close to home. One study of foodstore purchases in the central city area revealed that nearly 70 percent of the woman patronized stores within one to five blocks of their homes. Another study of food-stores indicated that for suburban locations the majority of customers lived within three miles of the stores, while the maximum trading area was five miles. For rural locations, the majority of consumers lived within a ten minute drive to the store, with the maximum trading area within a twenty minute drive. A West Coast supermarket chain wants a minimum of 3,500 homes within a mile-and-a-half radius of a shopping center before considering it for location. Research indicated that 80 percent of the customers of pizza carryouts lived within a mile of the establishments.

On the other hand, a retailer dealing in shopping goods can have a much wider trading area, Without a heavily trafficked location - but with the help of adequate promotion - this more expensive type of store can generate its own traffic density but easy accessibility from a residential area is a satisfactory site. The consumer buys these goods infrequently and deliberately plans these purchases. Consumers are willing to travel some distance to make shopping comparisons.

If you offer shopping goods, however, you should not locate too far away from your potential customers. One study of a discount department store showed that 79.6 percent of the shoppers lived within five miles of the store and another 16.1 percent lived within a ten-mile radius. The magnitude of the trading area for a shopping goods store can be determined by a customer survey, automobile license checks, sales slips, charge account records, store deliveries, and the extent of local newspaper circulation.

The same principles of location which are applicable to the walk-in specialty goods stores are appropriate for the drive-in facility. Because this type of retailer generates its own traffic, you can locate away from the major traffic arteries.

Planned Shopping Centers (Retail Store Locations)

Many merchants seek a retail location in a planned shopping center. Retailers in cities where downtown business has suffered extensive loss to shopping centers should perhaps consider locating in or near a center. The downtown area that suffers the most from the development of a shopping center is in a city of about 100,000 population, which is just large enough to support a center. Shopping centers have been classified into three different types: the neighborhood center, the community center, and the regional center.

The neighborhood center generally serves 7,500 to 20,500 people living within a six to ten minute drive from the center. The major store - and the prime traffic generator - in the center is a supermarket. The other stores in the center, which may include a drugstore, hardware store, bakery, and beauty shop, offer convenience goods and services, The best location for a specialty food store in the center is adjacent to the supermarket. Other stores should be grouped by the compatibility of their merchandise.

The community center usually serves 20,000 to 100,000 people living within a ten to twenty minute drive. The dominant store is generally a junior department store or a large variety store. The majority of the stores carry shopping goods such as wearing apparel and appliances. However, a number of the stores also offer convenience items. The apparel and furnishings stores should locate as close to the dominant store as possible. A supermarket in this type of center is best located at one end. This is so that the adjacent parking is less apt to be used for long periods by the shoppers in the other stores. An end site or a location near a major entry is also desirable for a drugstore. Because drugstores tend to maintain longer hours than the other stores, they should be in an easily accessible location and not surrounded by a number of dark stores at night. A service establishment, such as a dry-cleaner or a barbershop, which depends on a rapid turnover of traffic in the center, should locate where there is always available parking.

The regional center serves 100,000 to 200,000 people within a twenty to forty minute drive from the center. One or more department stores are its major tenants. Frequently, the center is an enclosed mall with department stores at both ends. This type of center emphasized shopping goods. These numerous shopping goods stores usually locate between the two major stores in order to take advantage of the traffic flow, Stores handling convenience goods generally locate at the edge of the center or near an entry to the mall where there is easily accessible parking. Service and repair shops are also usually located in these areas of the regional center.

8. How to Choose a Good Shopping Center Location

Retailers who seek new sites for their stores, or service shops should add the shopping center location to their lists of possible locations. When they do, however, they should be aware that the advantages of the shopping center for one type of retailing may be disadvantages for another.

The purpose of this Guide is to provide retailers with background information so that they can decide whether to locate their stores in shopping centers should such a decision be necessary. Among other things, it discusses the landlord-tenant relationship and the cost picture. Both of these factors are more complicated in shopping centers than in other locations.

Where you locate your store is one of your most important decisions. This fact is true whether you are opening a new store, starting a second outlet, or renewing your present lease. The problem is to find the right location for the right undertaking because a location can make or break a business.

Different stores have different locational requirements. You would not put a toy store in a retirement village or start a garden supply in a rental apartment house district. The customers you serve, the things they buy, the way they reach your store, the adjacent stores, and the neighborhood all bear upon the location. These factors must be related to the types and characteristics of shopping centers when you are considering a shopping center as a site.

Shopping Center Locations Characteristics

Shopping centers are distinctly different from the other two major locations - that is, downtown and local business strips. The shopping center building is pre-planned as a merchandising unit for interplay among tenants. Its site is deliberately selected by the developer for easy access to pull customers from a trade area. It has on-site parking as a common feature of the layout. The amount of parking space is directly related to the retail area.

Customers like the shopping center's convenience. They drive in, park, walk to their destination in relative safety and speed. Some shopping centers also provide weather protection and most provide an atmosphere created for shopping comfort. For the customer, the shopping center has great appeal.

For the merchant making a decision whether or not to locate in a shopping center, these "plus" characteristics must be related to the limitations placed upon you as a tenant. In a shopping center, a tenant is part of a merchant team. As such, you must pay your pro rata share of the budget for the team effort. You must keep store hours, light your windows, and place your signs within established rules.

What Are Your Chances of Finding a Good Shopping Center Location

Whether or not a small retailer can get into a particular shopping center depends on the market and management. A small shopping center may need only one children's shoe store, for example, while a regional center may expect enough business for several. The management aspect is simple to state: Developers and owners of shopping centers look for successful retailers.

In finding tenants whose line of goods will meet the needs of the desired market, the developer-owner first signs on a prestige merchant as the lead tenant. Then, the developer selects other types of stores that will complement each other. In this way, a "tenant mix" offers a varied array of merchandise. Thus, the center's competitive strength is bolstered against other centers as well as supplying the market area's needs.

To finance a center, the developer needs major leases from companies with strong credit

ratings. The developer's own lenders favor
tenant rosters that include the triple-A ratings
of national chains. However, local merchants
with good business records and proven
understanding of the local markets have a
good chance of being considered by a shopping
center developer.

But even so, a small independent retailer can
sometimes play "hard to get." When most
spaces are filled, the developer may need you
to help fill the rest of them.

If you are considering a shopping center for a
first-store venture you may have trouble. Your
financial backing and merchandising
experience may be unproved to the owner-
developer. Your problem is to convince the
developer that the new store has a reasonable
chance of success and will help the "tenant
mix."

What Can the a Shopping Center Location Do for You?

Suppose that the owner-developer of a
shopping center asks you to be a tenant. In
considering the offer, you would need to make
sure of what you can do in the center. What
rules will there be on your operation? In
exchange for the rules, what will the center do
for you?

Even more important, you must consider the
trade area, the location of your competition,

and the location of your space in the center. These factors help to determine how much business you can expect to do in the center.

In a neighborhood shopping center, the leading tenant is a supermarket or drug store. The typical leasable space is 150,000 square feet but may range form 30,000 to 100,000 square feet. The typical site area is 10 to 30 acres. The minimum trade population is 2,500 to 40,000.

In a community shopping center, the leading tenant is a variety/junior department store or discount department store. The typical leasable space is 150,000 square feet but may range form 100,000 to 300,000 square feet. The typical site area is 10 to 30 acres. The minimum trade population is 40,000 to 150,000.

In a regional shopping center, the leading tenant is one or more full-line department stores. The typical leasable space is 400,000 square feet with a range from 300,000 to more than 1,000,000 square feet. They typical site area is 30 to 50 acres. The minimum trade population is 150,000 or more. When the regional center exceeds 750,000 square feet and includes three or more department stores, it becomes a SUPER-REGIONAL CENTER.

The Centers Location. In examining the center's location, look for answers to questions such as these:

Can you hold old customers and attract new ones?

Would the center offer the best sales volume potential for your kind of merchandise?

Can you benefit enough from the center's access to a market? If so, can you produce the appeal that will make the center's customers come to your store?

Can you deal with your logical competition?

To help answer such question, you need to check out; (1) the trade area and its growth prospects; (2) the general income level in the trade area; (3) the number of households; and (4) the share of various age groups in the population. If your line is clothes for young women, for example, you would not want to locate in a center whose market area contains a high percentage of retired persons.

Make your own analysis of the market which the developer expects to reach. In this respect, money for professional help is well spent, especially when the research indicates that the center is not right for your type of operation.

Your Space. Determine where your space will be. Your location in the center is important. Do you need to be in the main flow of customers as they pass between the stores with the greatest customer pull? Who will be your neighbors? What will be their effect on your sales?

How much space is also important. Using your experience, you can determine the amount of space you will need to handle the sales volume you expect to have in the shopping center. And, of course, the amount of space will determine your rent. Many merchants need to rethink their space requirements when locating in a shopping center. Rents are typically much higher and, therefore, space must be used very efficiently.

"Total Rent". In most non-shopping center locations rent is a fixed amount which has no relationship to sales volume. In shopping centers the "rent" is usually stated as a minimum guaranteed rent per square foot of leased area against a percentage. Typically, while this is between 5 and 7 percent of gross sales, it varies by type of business and other factors. This means that if the rents as calculated by the percentage of sales is higher than the guaranteed rent, the higher amount is the rent. If it is lower than the guaranteed rent, then the guaranteed rent is the amount paid.

But this guarantee is not the end. In addition, you may have to pay dues to the center's merchant association. You may have to pay for maintenance of common areas. Consider your rent, then, in terms of "total rent." If, and when, this is "total rent" is more than your present rent, your space in the center of course, will have to draw sales enough to justify the added cost.

Finishing out. Generally the owner furnishes the bare space. You do the "finishing out" at your own expense. In completing your store to suit your needs, you pay for light fixtures, counters, shelves, painting, floor coverings. In addition, you may have to install your own heating and cooling units. (Your lease should be long enough to pay out your "finishing out" expense).

An innovation is the "tenant allowance." By this system, landlords provide a cost allowance towards the completion of space. It is for store fronts, ceiling treatment, and wall coverings. The allowance is a percentage of their cost and is spelled out in a dollar amount in the lease.

Some developers help tenants plan store fronts, exterior signs, and interior color schemes. They provide this service to insure store fronts that add to the center's image rather than subtracting from it.

Types of Shopping Centers Locations

Because each planned shopping center is built around a major tenant, centers are classed, in part according to this leading tenant. According to tenant makeup and size, there are three types: neighborhood, community, and regional.

Neighborhood. The supermarket or the drugstore is the leading tenant in a neighborhood center. This type is the smallest in size among shopping centers. It caters to the convenience needs of a neighborhood.

Community. Variety, junior department stores or discount department stores lead in the next bigger type - the community center. Here, you find room also for more specialty shops, need for wider price ranges, for greater style assortments, and for more impulse-sale items. In recent years the community center has also been designed around the home improvement department store which combine hardware, lumber, electrical plumbing, flooring, building materials, garden supplies, and a variety of other goods under one roof. The shops that are grouped around this type of anchor tend to be similar in character and may include custom kitchen and bath shops, upholstery, bedding, drapery, and other such shops. While this type of center tends to meet the Community Shopping Center definition as to floor area and site size, its market may be more like a regional center.

Regional. The department store, with its prestige, is the leader in the regional center. When you find that a second or third department store is also locating in such a center, you will know the site has been selected to draw from the widest possible market area. Super-Regional centers have been developed with as many as 5 department stores. You will find too, that the smaller tenants are picked to offer a range of goods and services approaching the appeal once found only downtown.

The latest development in regional shopping centers is the enclosed mall. This type of center is designed to shut out the weather and to serve a larger trade area than other regional centers. Customers enjoy the open store fronts, the easy entrance, and the "all-weather" shopping. Tenants enjoy more center-wide promotions because of weather control.

An enclosed air-conditioned mall enables you to merchandise the full width of your store. The whole store becomes a display area, eliminating window backing and expensive display settings. You can rely on sliding doors or an overhead open drop grill for locking up the store.

If you are considering a mall, you should weigh the benefits against costs. At the outset, it may be difficult to measure savings, such as the elimination of store fronts, against costs, for example the cost for heating and air-conditioning in the enclosed mall.

Specialty Theme Shopping Centers. In addition to the three major categories of shopping centers new types of centers are evolving that have been called specialty or theme centers. In general these centers do not have a major anchor tenant. There is a greater percentage of restaurants and specialty food stores, the other stores tend to be highly specialized with more imported goods, custom crafted goods, designer clothes etc. Also a greater number of the merchants are independents. Unusual and interesting architectural design is a normal characteristic and frequently a tourist market rather than a resident market exists.

9. Retail Marketing Essentials

This chapter is a Retail Marketing Management Plan Checklist for the owner-manager of a retail business. The questions cover areas that under-gird retail marketing as well as deal with obvious aspects like customer analysis, buying, pricing, and promotion. You can use it to evaluate your current status and, perhaps, to rethink certain decisions.

If your retail marketing management is to be successful in retail over the long run, it must satisfy the needs and desires of its present and potential Customers. Sound Buying means knowing where to buy, what to buy, how much to buy, and how to place an order. This requires familiarity with old and new products, adequate and working with suppliers in ways that benefit the store. In Pricing, you need to understand the market forces affecting your business, plan the price policies that you will follow, and know whether or not your pricing policies meet State and Federal regulations.

You need to be familiar with various types of Promotion and when, where, and how to use them. In addition, a credit program or other special customer services can be attractions.

Under the heading of Management goes the establishment of both long- and short-range goals. How you set up your organization and how you communicate with your employees are crucial factors in the accomplishment of your goals. Of equal importance to good management is the ability to keep and make use of accurate Financial Records. It also pays to examine your Insurance coverage in various areas.

In answering the following questions, you will be reminded of what you may still need to do to round out all marketing aspects of your business.

Retail Customer Analysis

Who are your target customers and what are they seeking from you?

Have you estimated the total market you share with competition?

Should you try to appeal to this entire market rather than a segment(s)?

If you concentrate on a segment, is it large enough to be profitable?

Have you looked into possible changes taking place among your target customers which could significantly affect your business?

Can you foresee changes in the makeup of your store's neighborhood?

Are incomes in the community apt to be stable?

Is the community's population subject to fluctuation?

Do you stress a special area of appeal, such as lower prices, better quality, wider selection, convenient hours?

Do you ask your customers for suggestions on ways to improve your operation?

Do you use "want slips"?

Do you belong to a trade association?

Do you subscribe to important trade publications?

Have you considered using a consumer questionnaire to aid you in determining customer needs?

Do you visit market shows and conventions to help anticipate customer wants?

Do most of your customers buy on weekends?

Do sales increase in the evening?

Do the majority of your customers prefer buying on credit?

Retail Buying

Have you a merchandise budget (planned purchases) for each season?

Does it take into consideration planned sales for the season?

Does it achieve a planned stock turnover?

Have you broken it down by departments or merchandise classifications?

Have you a formal plan for deciding what to buy and from whom?

Have you a system for reviewing new items coming onto the market?

Have you considered using a basic stock list or a model stock plan in your buying?

Are you using some sort of unit control system?

Do you keep track of the success of your buying decisions in previous years to aid you in next year's buying?

Do you attempt to consolidate your purchases with two or three principal suppliers?

Have you a useful supplier evaluation system for determining their performance?

Have you established a planned gross margin for your firm's operation and are you buying so as to achieve it?

Retail Pricing

Have you established a set of pricing policies?

Have you determined whether to price below, at, or above the market?

Do you set specific markups for each product?

Do you set markups for each product categories?

Do you use a one-price policy rather than bargain with customers?

Do you offer discounts for quality purchases, or to special groups?

Do you set prices to cover full costs on every sale?

Have you developed policy on when to take markdowns and how large?

Do the prices you have established earn planned gross margin?

Do you clearly understand the market forces affecting your pricing methods?

Do you know which products are slow movers and which are fast?

Do you take into consideration when pricing?

Do you know which products are prices sensitive to your customers, that is, when a slight increase in price will lead to a big drop-off in demand?

Do you know the maximum price customers will pay for certain products?

If the prices on some products are dropped too low, do buyers hesitate?

Is there a specific time of year when your competitors have sales?

Do your customers expect sales at certain times?

Have you determined whether or not a series of sales is better than one clearance sale?

Do you know what role you want price to play in your overall retailing strategy?

Are you influenced by competitor's price changes?

Are there restrictions regarding prices you can charge?

Do any of your suppliers set a minimum standard at which it can be sold?

Does your State have fair trade practice acts which require you to mark up your merchandise by a minimum percentage?

Are there any State regulations on how long "close-out" sales can be advertised?

Are you sure you know all the regulations affecting your retail business, such as two-for-one sales and the like?

Do you issue "rain-checks" to customers when sale items are sold out so they can purchase later at sale price?

Retail Promotion

Are you familiar with the strengths and weaknesses of various promotional methods?

Have you considered how each type might be used for your firm?

Do you know which of your items can be successfully advertised?

Do you know which can be sold best by demonstrations?

Do you know when it is profitable to use institutional advertising?

Do you know when product advertising is better?

Do you know which of the media (radio, television, newspapers, yellow pages, handbills) can most effectively reach your target group?

Do you know what can and cannot be said in your ads (Truth in Advertising requirements)?

Can you make use of direct mail?

Is a good mailing list available?

Are your promotional efforts fairly regular?

Do you concentrate them on certain seasons?

Are certain periods of the week better than others?

Is there available financial or technical assistance which you can use to enhance your promotional efforts?

Can you get help from local newspapers, radio, or television?

Are cooperative advertising funds available from suppliers?

Do you tie your local efforts to your supplier's national program?

Do you join with other merchants in area-wide programs?

Have you looked for ratios to estimate what comparable firms are spending on promotion?

Do you study the advertising of other successful retail firms, as well as of your competitors?

Have you some ways of measuring the success of the various promotional programs you are using?

Are your products displayed to maximize their appeal within the store?

Do you know which of your items have unusual eye appeal and can be effective in displays?

Have you figured out the best locations in the store for displays?

Are you making use of window displays to attract customers?

If you use multi-tiered display stands or gondolas, do you know which shelves are the best sellers?

Have you a schedule for changing various displays?

Do you know which items are bought on "impulse" and therefore should be placed in high traffic areas?

Where price is important, do you make sure the price cards are easy to read?

Do your suppliers offer financing of accounts receivable, floor planning, and so forth?

Do you know what type of credit program (if any) you should offer?

Does the nature of your operation require some type of credit for your customers?

Have you discussed credit operations with your local credit bureau?

Would a credit program be a good sales tool?

Is a credit program of your own desirable?

Have you looked into other programs of credit cards?

If you set up your own credit program, do you know what standards you should use in determining which customers can receive credit, for what time periods, and in what amounts?

Do you know all of the costs involved?

Will the interest you charge pay for these costs?

Do you know about the Fair Credit Reporting Act?

Are you familiar with the Truth-in-Lending legislation?

Have you determined a safe percentage off your retail business to have on credit program with your accountant and attorney?

Do you offer some special customer services?

If you offer delivery service, do you own your vehicles?

Have you considered leasing them instead?

Have you thought about using commercial delivery service?

Do you charge for delivery?

If not, do you know how to work the delivery expenses into the selling price of your products?

Have you a policy for handling merchandise returned by customers?

Have you considered certain obligations to your community, in terms of charitable contributions, donations for school functions, ads in school yearbooks?

Do you participate in activities of your chamber of commerce, merchants' association, better business bureau, or other civic organizations?

Retail Marketing Management

Have you developed a set of plans for the year's operations?

Do your plans provide methods to deal with competition?

Do they contain creative approaches to solving problems?

Are they realistic?

Are they stated in such a way that you know when they have been achieved?

Have you a formal plan for setting aside money to meet any quarterly tax payments?

Are you organized effectively?

Are job descriptions and authority for responsibilities clearly stated?

Does your organizational structure minimize duplication of effort and maximize the use of each employee's skills?

Do employees understand how they will be rated for promotion and salary increases?

Does your wage schedule meet the local rate for similar work and retain competent employees?

Would you or some of your employees profit by taking business education courses offered at local schools?

Will training help your employees achieve better results?

Do your experienced employees help train new and part-time employees?

Have you good working conditions?

Do you use positive personal leadership techniques like being impartial, giving words of encouragement and congratulations, and listening to complaints?

Are you familiar with the Fair Labor Standards Act as it applies to minimum wages, overtime payments, and child labor?

Do you avoid all forms of discrimination in your employment practices?

Do you have a formal program for motivating employees?

Have you taken steps to minimize shoplifting and internal theft?

Have you an effective system for communicating with employees?

Are they informed on those plans and results that effect their work?

Do you hold regular meetings that include all personnel?

Do your employees have their own bulletin board for both material you need to post and items they with to post?

Have the "rules and regulations" been explained to each employee?

Does each employee have a written copy?

Is each employee familiar with other positions and departments?

Do you have an "open door" policy in your office?

Retail Financial Analysis and Control

Have you established a useful accounting system?

Do you know the minimum amount of records you need for good control?

Do you know all the records you should keep to aid you in meeting your tax obligations on time?

Do your Sales records give you the key information you need to make sound decisions?

Can you separate cash sales from charge sales?

Can sales be broken down by department?

Can they be broken down by merchandise classification?

Do they provide a way to assess each salesperson's performance?

Do your Inventory records give you the key information you need to make sound decisions?

Do they show how much you have invested in merchandise without the necessity of a physical inventory?

Do you know the difference between inventory valuation at cost and at market?

can you tell which one shows a loss in the period earned?

Can you tell which one conserves cash?

Do you understand the pros and cons of the cost method of inventory accounting versus the retail method?

Have you found an accounting method that shows the amount of inventory shortages in a year?

Do your Expense records give you the key information you need to make sound decisions?

Do you know which expense items you have the greatest control over?

Are the records sufficiently detailed to identify where the money goes?

Can you detect those expenses not necessary to the successful operation of your business?

Do you effectively use the information on your profit and loss statement and balance sheet?

Do you analyze monthly financial statements?

can you interpret your financial statements in terms of how you did last year and whether you met this year's goals?

Do your financial statements compare favorably with other similar businesses in terms of sales, cost of sales, and expenses?

Are you under-capitalized?

Have you borrowed more than you can easily pay back out of profits?

Can you see ways to improve your profit position by improving your gross margin?

Do you use the information contained in your financial statements to prepare a cash budget?

Insurance

Have you adequate insurance coverage?

Do you have up-to-date fire coverage on both your building equipment and inventory?

Does your liability insurance cover bodily injuries as well as such problems as libel and slander suits?

Are you familiar with your obligations to employees under both common law and worker's compensation?

Do you spread your insurance coverage among a number of agents and take the risk of overlapping coverage or gaps which may raise questions as to which firm is responsible?

Has your insurance agent shown you how you can cut premiums in areas like fleet automobile coverage, proper classification of employees under worker's compensation, cutting back on seasonal inventory insurance?

Have you looked into other insurance coverage, such as business interruption insurance or criminal insurance?

Do you have some fringe benefit insurance for your employees (group life, group health, or retirement insurance)?

These questions are meant to help you analyze your retail Marketing operation from the marketing viewpoint. You should know the strengths of your business and products. You must also know the real problems you are up against. Your business depends on your good sense and management foresight. You must adapt to new markets, product changes, and be innovative to keep your business growing.

10. How to Set Prices for Optimal Profitability

This Setting Prices in a Retail Store Guide is a checklist for the owner-manager of a retail business. These 51 questions probe the consideration - from markup to pricing strategy to adjustments - that lead to correct set prices decisions. You can use this checklist to establish setting prices in your new store, or you can use it to periodically review your established pricing policy.

A retailer's set prices influence the quantities of various items that consumers will buy, which in turn affects total revenue and profit. Hence, correct setting prices decisions are a key to successful retail management. With this in mind, the following checklist of 52 questions has been developed to assist retailers in making systematic, informed decisions regarding pricing strategies and tactics.

This checklist should be especially useful to a new retailer who is making pricing decisions for the first time. However, established retailers, including successful ones, can also benefit from this Guide. They may use it as a reminder of all the individual pricing decisions they should review periodically. And, it may also be used in training new employees who will have pricing authority.

The Central Concept of Setting Prices

A major step toward making a profit in retailing is selling merchandise for more than it cost you. This difference between cost of merchandise and retail price is called markup (or occasionally markon). From an arithmetic standpoint, markup is calculated as follows:

Dollar markup = Retail price - Cost of the merchandise.

Percentage markup =

Dollar markup

‾‾‾‾‾‾‾‾‾‾‾‾

Retail price

If an item cost $6.50 and you feel consumers will buy it at $10.00, the dollar markup is $3.50 (which is $10.00 - $6.59). Going one step further, the percentage markup is 35 percent (which is $3.50 divided by $10.00). Anyone involved in retail pricing should be as knowledgeable about formulas as about the name and preferences of his or her best customer!

Two other key points about markup should be mentioned. First, the cost of merchandise used in calculating markup consists of the base invoice for the merchandise plus any transportation charges minus any quantity and cash discounts given by the seller.

Second, retail price, rather than cost, is ordinarily used in calculating percentage markup. The reason for this is that when other operating figures such as wages, advertising expenses, and profits are expressed as a percentage, all are being based on retail price rather than cost of the merchandise being sold.

Target Consumers and the Retailing Mix

In this section, your attention is directed to price as it relates to your potential customers. These questions examine your merchandise, location, promotion, and customer services that will be combined with price in attempting to satisfy customers and make a profit. After some questions, brief commentary is provided.

1. Is the relative price of this item very important to your target consumers?

The importance of setting prices depends on the specific product and on the specific individual. Some shoppers are very price conscious. Others want convenience and knowledgeable sales personnel. Because of these variations, you need to learn about your customers' desires in relation to different products. Having sales personnel seek feedback from shoppers is a good starting point.

2. Are set prices based on estimates of the number of units that consumers will demand at various price levels?

Demand-orientated pricing such as this is superior to cost-orientated pricing. In the cost approach, a predetermined amount is added to the cost of the merchandise, whereas the demand approach considers what consumers are willing to pay.

3. Have you established a price range for the product?

The cost of merchandise will be at one end of the price range and the level above which consumers will not buy the product at the other end.

4. Have you considered what price strategies would be compatible with your store's total retailing mix that includes merchandise, location, promotion, and services

5. Will trade-ins be accepted as part of the purchase price on items such as appliances and television sets?

Supplier and Competitor considerations in setting prices

This set of questions looks outside your firm to two factors that you cannot directly control - suppliers and competitors.

6. Do you have final pricing authority?

With the repeal of fair trade laws, "yes" answers will be more common than in previous years. Still, a supplier can control retail prices by refusing to deal with non-conforming stores (a tactic which may be illegal) or by selling to you on consignment.

7. Do you know what direct competitors are doing price-wise?

8. Do you regularly review competitor's ads to obtain information on their prices?

9. Is your store large enough to employ either a full-time or a part-time comparison shopper?

These three questions emphasize the point that you must watch competitors' prices so that your prices will not be far out of line - too high or too low - without good reason. Of, course, there may be a good reason for the out-of-the-ordinary prices, such as seeking a special price image.

A Price Level Strategy

Selecting a general level of prices in relation to competition is a key strategic decision, perhaps the most important.

10. Should your overall strategy be to sell at prevailing market price levels?

The other alternatives are an above-the-market strategy or a below-the-market strategy.

11. Should competitor's temporary price reductions ever be matched?

12. Could private-brand merchandise be obtained in order to avoid direct price competition?

Calculating Planned Initial Markup in setting prices

In this section you will have to look inside your business, taking into account sales, expenses, and profits before setting prices. The point is that your initial markup must be large enough to cover anticipated expenses and reductions and still produce a satisfactory profit.

13. Have you estimated sales, operating expenses, and reductions for the next selling season?

14. Have you established a profit objective for the next selling season

15. Given estimated sales, expenses, and reductions, have you planned initial markup?

This figure is calculated with the following formula:

Initial markup percentage =

Operating expenses + Reductions + Profit

Net sales + Reductions

Reductions consist of markdowns, stock shortages, and employee and customer discounts. The following example uses dollar amounts, but the estimates can also be percentages, and if the retailer desires a $4,000 profit, initial markup percentage can be calculated:

Initial markup percentage =

$$\frac{\$34,000 + \$6,000 + \$4,000}{\$94,000 + \$6,000} = 44\%$$

The resulting figure, 44 percent in this example, indicates what size markup is needed on the average in order to make the desired profits.

16 Would it be appropriate to have different initial markup figures for various lines of merchandise or service?

You would seriously consider this when some lines have much different characteristics than others. For instance, a clothing retailer might logically have different initial markup figures for suits, shirts, and pants, and accessories. (Various merchandise characteristics are covered in an upcoming section.) You may want those items with the highest turnover rates to carry the lowest initial markup.

Set Prices Store Policies

Having calculated an initial markup figure, you could proceed to set prices on your merchandise. But an important decision such as this should not be rushed. Instead, you should consider additional factors which suggest what would be the best price.

Policies are written guidelines indicating appropriate methods or actions in different methods or actions in different situations. If established with care, they can save you time in decision making and provide for consistent treatment of shoppers. Specific policy areas that you should consider are as follows:

18. Will a one-price system, under which the same price is charged every purchaser of a particular item, be used on all items?

The alternative is to negotiate price with consumers

19. Will odd-ending prices such as $1.98 and $44.95, be more appealing to your customers than never-ending price

20. Will consumers buy more if multiple pricing, such as 2 for $8.50, is used?

21. Should any leader offerings (selected products with quite, low less profitable prices) be used?

22.Have the characteristics of an effective leader offering been considered?

Ordinarily, a leader offering needs the following characteristics to accomplish its purpose of generating much shopper traffic: used by most people, bought frequently, very familiar regular price, and not a large expenditure for consumers.

23. Will price lining, the practice of setting up distinct points (such as $5.00, $7.50 and $10.00) and then marking all related merchandise at these points, be used?

24 Would price lining by means of zones (such as $5.00 - $7.50 and $12.50 - $15.00) be more appropriate than price points?

25. Will cent-off coupons be used in newspaper ads or mailed to selected consumers on any occasion?

26. Would periodic special sales, combining reduced prices and heavier advertising, be consistent with the store image you are seeking?

27. Do certain items have greater appeal than others when they are part of a special sale?

28 Has the impact of various sale items on profit been considered?

Sales prices may mean little or no profit on these items. Still, the special sales may contribute to total profits by bringing in shoppers who may also buy some regular-price (and profitable) merchandise and by attracting new customers. Also, you should avoid featuring items that require a large amount of labor, which in turn would reduce or erase profits. For instance, according to this criterion, shirts would be a better special sales item than men's suits that often require free alterations.

29. Will "rain checks" be issued to consumers who come in for special-sale merchandise that is temporarily out of stock?

You should give particular attention to this decision since rain checks are required in some situations. Your lawyer or the regional Federal Trade Commission office should be consulted for specific advice regarding whether rain checks are needed in the special sales you plan.

Nature of the Merchandise

In this section you will be considering how selected characteristics of particular merchandise affect planned initial markup.

30. Did you get a "good deal" on the wholesale price of this merchandise?

31. Is this item at the peak of its popularity?

32. Are handling and selling costs relatively great due to the product being bulky, having a low turnover rate, and requiring much personal selling, installation, or alterations?

33. Are relatively large levels of reductions expected due to markdowns, spoilage, breakage, or theft?

With respect to the preceding four questions, "Yes" answers suggest the possibility of or need for larger-than-normal initial markups. For example, very fashionable clothing often will carry a higher markup than basic clothing such as underwear because the particular fashion may suddenly lose its appeal to consumers.

34. Will customer services such as delivery, alterations, gift wrapping, and installation be free of charge to customers?

The alternative is to charge for some or all of these services

Environmental Consideration

The questions in this section focus your attention on three factors outside your business, namely economic conditions, laws, and consumerism.

35. Are economic conditions in your trading area abnormal?

Consumers tend to be price-conscious when the economy is depressed, suggesting that lower-than-normal markups may be needed to be competitive. On the other hand, shoppers are less price-conscious when the economy is booming, which would permit larger markups on a selective basis.

36. Are the ways in which prices are displayed and promoted compatible with consumerism, one part of which has been a call for more straightforward price information?

37. If yours is a grocery store, it is feasible to use unit pricing in which the item's cost per some standard measure is indicated?

Having asked (and hopefully answered) more than three dozen questions, you are indeed ready to establish retail prices. When you have decided on an appropriate percentage markup, 35 percent on a garden hose, for example, the next step is to determine what percentage of the still unknown retail price is represented by the cost figure. The basic markup formula is simply rearranged to do this:

Cost = Retail price - Markup

Cost = 100% - 35% = 65%

Then the dollar cost, say $3.25 for the garden hose, is plugged in to the following formula to arrive at the retail price:

Retail price =

$$\text{Retail price} = \frac{\text{Dollar cost}}{\text{Percentage cost}} =$$

$$\frac{\$3.25}{65\% \text{ (or .65)}} = \$5.00$$

One other consideration is necessary:

38. Is the retail price consistent with your planned initial markups?

Set Prices Adjustments

It would be ideal if all items sold at their original retail prices. But we know that things are not always ideal. Therefore, a section on price adjustments is necessary.

39. Are additional markups called for because wholesale prices have increased or because an item's low price causes consumers to question its quality?

40. Should employees be given purchase discounts?

41. Should any groups of customers, such as students or senior citizens, be given purchase discounts?

42. When markdowns appear necessary, have you first considered other alternatives such as retaining price but changing another element of the retailing mix or storing the merchandise until the next selling season?

43. Has an attempt been made to identify causes of markdown so that steps can be taken to minimize the number of avoidable buying, selling, and pricing errors that cause markdowns?

44. Has the relationship between timing and size of markdowns been taken into account?

In general, markdowns taken early in the selling season or shortly after sales slow down can be smaller than late markdowns. Whether an early or late markdown would be more appropriate in a particular situation depends on how many consumers might still be interested in the product, the size of the initial markup and the amount remaining in stock.

45. Would a schedule or automatic markdowns after merchandise has been in stock for specified intervals be appropriate?

46. Is the size of the markdown "just enough" to stimulate purchases?

This question stresses the point that you have to observe the effects of markdowns so that you can know what size markdowns are "just enough" for different kinds of merchandise.

47. Has a procedure been worked out for markdowns on price-lined merchandise?

48. Is the markdown price calculated from the off-retail percentage?

This question gets you into the arithmetic of markdowns. Usually, you first tentatively decide on the percentage amount price must be marked down to excite consumers. For example, if you think a 25 percent markdown will be necessary to sell a lavender sofa, the dollar amount of the markdown is calculated as follows:

Dollar markdown = Off-retail percentage x Previous retail price

Dollar markdown = 25% (or .25) x $500 = $125

Then the markdown price is obtained by subtracting the dollar markdown from the previous retail price. Hence, the sofa would be $375.00 after taking the markdown.

49. Has cost of the merchandise been considered before setting the markdown price?

This is not to say that a markdown price should never be lower than cost, on the contrary, a price that low may be your only hope of generating some revenue from the item. But cost should be considered to make sure that below-cost markdown prices are the exception in your store rather than being so common that your total profits are really hurt.

50. Have procedures for recording the dollar amounts, percentages, and probable causes of markdowns been set up?

Markdown analysis can provide information for assist in calculating planned initial markup, in decreasing errors that cause markdowns, and in evaluating suppliers.

51. Have you marked the calendar for a periodic review of your pricing decisions?

Rather than making careless pricing decisions, this checklist should help you lay a solid foundation of effective prices as you try to build retail.

11. How to Improve Personal Selling in Your Store

This chapter discusses Sales Skills and Techniques. An important ingredient in the successful business is good sales skills. Without it, many sales are lost - sales that may mean the difference between success and failure. This Guide tells how you can train yourself and your employees to Boost Sales Techniques.

To many customers, the salesperson is the business. Therefore, if the sales personnel are good, the business if good. But if the sales personnel are bad, then so is the firm. Although important to all businesses, effective sales personnel are especially important to small businesses. Why? Because, it is difficult for a small business to compete with the big firms on things like assortment, price and promotion. Sales effort, on the other hand, is one place where the small product or service retail business can compete with larger competitors - and win.

Effective sales skills doesn't happen by accident. The small entrepreneur must work to achieve a high level of sales effectiveness in his or her business. In order to work toward this goal, the business person should be aware of the different types of salespersons, the sales process, and the attributes of effective salespersons. Applying such knowledge to a business situation should result in the desired goal of effective sales personnel - the competitive edge.

It is important to note that retailing may involve sales services instead of products. Appliance repair, beauty shop, lawn service, and photography studio are all examples of service retailing. Even though services are intangible, personal, non-standardized, and perishable when compared to products, they are sold by retailers either alone or in conjunction with the products. The effective sales of services has the potential to give a business a competitive advantage.

Types of Salespersons

Order-Handler

The ticket-taker at the concert, the checker at the food store - these salespeople are working in a routine sales environment. But due to the nature of their jobs, they will be asked numerous questions by customers as well as hear complaints about prices and service. A knowledgeable person with a pleasant personality is especially needed for this job, because this is usually the person who is dealing with the customer when the customer's money (payment) is received.

Order-Taker

more creativity is found in this job as compared to the order-handler. The counter attendant at the fast food restaurant may take the order and then suggest that the customer might also wish to buy a hot apple turnover. Pleasant personality, fast service, and suggestion selling on the part of the order-taker can result in many additional sales.

Order-Getter

For many businesses, the heart of the sales process rests with the creative selling efforts of their salespeople. Of course, one of the greatest problems is that there are numerous order-handlers and order-takers in sales positions that should have order-getters for optimum sales effectiveness. Clothing, furniture, jewelry, and appliances are just some of the many items that call for order-getters (a person who can handle a transaction, take an order, and, most importantly, get an order). As for services, the home security salesperson, for example, who calls on a prospect because it is observed that the house has no dead bolt locks, is making that special effort to be an order-getter. Even though all sales situations do not call for order-getters, all salespeople will be called upon to sell creatively from time to time. It is for this reason that all sales personnel need to have a working knowledge of the creative selling process.

Creative Sales skills Process

the creative sales skills process consists of eight steps, none of which is less important than any other if the process is to be effective. It should be emphasized to all employees that all steps are vital to the achievement of effective sales.

1. Pre-Customer Contact

A smart builder would not attempt to build a house without a good foundation. Likewise, a businessperson should not place people on the sales floor or telephone until these people know the business, merchandise, services, and customers. Before any contact is made with the customer, every salesperson should know:

Policies, Procedures, and Rules. Have these in writing for all employees to see and to know.

Operation of Equipment. No matter whether the register is electronic or mechanical, the time to learn how it works is not after a sale while the customer waits for the change.

Target Market Knowledge. The better salesperson knows something of the likes and dislikes of the firms primary customers. The business operator should tell all sales personnel about the business's customers and their lifestyles. Tell the salespeople about customer's interests and their ability to buy.

Product Knowledge. A salesperson gains confidence by knowing about the products and services he or she is sales. If a person sells shoes, it helps to know the merchandise as well as how to fit them. If a person sells building materials, the sales job is probably more effective if the salesperson can also help answer questions about home repairs. It helps the person who sell clothes to know something about fabrics and current fashions. If the person is in the lawn service business, that person should know about lawn care. Most sales personnel will not take the initiative to acquire product on their own. It is management's responsibility to encourage employees to gain product and service knowledge. Management should make such knowledge available to them.

2. Prospecting

Although not appropriate to every sales situation, prospecting should be used whenever possible. Essentially, prospecting involves not waiting for the customer to show up at a store or to phone about a service. It is concerned with taking the initiative by going to the customer with a product or service idea. Prospecting may be of two types: new or regular customer prospecting.

New Customer Prospecting. A salesperson sees that a person is getting married. Action is taken on this knowledge by contacting the person and telling her about appropriate items (or services) that might be of assistance to a new bride. By using newspapers and personal contacts, a salesperson can take the initiative to contact and create new customers.

Regular Customer Prospecting. A firm's best prospects are its current customers. A salesperson should make a practice of calling regular customers on a periodic basis to tell them about products or services. "Hello, Mrs. Anderson, I just wanted to tell you about the new shipment of dresses that we received today. As I unpacked them, I saw several that made me think of you." Prospecting with regular customers works! All salespeople should be encouraged to prospect by phone and in-person whenever they see regular customers. A word of caution must be emphasized. Don't go to the well too often. Prospecting with the same regular customer on a frequent basis can make prospecting lose the special feeling that it can create in customers. Do not overuse it.

3. Initial Contact

The most effective way to close a sale is to open it on a positive note. Unfortunately, most sales do not open this way. The typical initial store contact begins in this manner:

Clerk: "May I help you?"

Customer: "No thank you, I'm just looking."

This ritual leaves much to be desired. Why? It is an automatic statement that shows no creativity on the part of the salesperson. Also, because the customer has heard the statement many times, his or her response is usually given without thinking what was said. Every salesperson should be challenged to treat each customer as an individual by responding differently to each customer.

Initial contact also means responding to customers when they enter the sales area even when they cannot be waited upon immediately. Salespeople should be instructed to tell waiting customers that, "I'll be with you in a moment." Such actions will reduce the number of customers who leave without being served. When the employee is free to help the waiting customer, the initial comment should be, "Thank you for waiting." A courteous, creative initial contact with the customer can go a long way to promote sales.

4. Presentation of Merchandise (Presentation Sales Skills)

In presenting merchandise (or services) to the customer, the salesperson should use product knowledge to best advantage. How?

Buyer Benefits. Although it is good to talk about the lawnmower's 3.5 horsepower mower, customers may be more interested in hearing how fast the lawnmower will cut the grass. Product knowledge is important but the

HOW TO OPEN A STORE

salesperson must remember what makes the customer buy. Clothes may be made of durable fabrics but it is also important to stress the implied benefit that they will also appeal to the opposite sex. Sell benefits!

Customer Involvement. Product knowledge can be used to get customer involvement. Show the customer several features of the digital watch and then have the customer put it on and work it. If the interest is there, it will be hard for the customer to take off the watch so that the salesperson can put it back into the case. The best way to present many products is to get involvement. Want to sell dance lessons? Get the customer on the dance floor and let the fun of dancing do some of the sales. The same is true with clothes, perfume, sports equipment, and almost anything else.

Limit the Choices. If during the sales presentation more than three items are in front of the customer, the chances of a sale are reduced while the possibility of shoplifting is increased. If, for example, the salesperson continues to carry dresses into the fitting room for the customer to try without removing any from the consideration, the customer will likely not buy any because of the inability to decide from among so many choices. Also, with so many items under study, the clerk may lose track of how many items are in the fitting room. It is possible that some may be put on under the customer's clothes while the clerk is not present, thereby resulting in an expensive experience for the store. Likewise, if a travel agency attempts to sell a customer a Caribbean cruise, the chances of making the sale will diminish if too many trip options are presented. Unless there is a definite reason for an exception, the rule of three (never show more than three choices at one time) should be followed whenever merchandise is presented. Limited choices have been found to promote sales.

Use Showmanship. In presenting merchandise to the customer, encourage all personnel to be creative. Be enthusiastic about the merchandise. Hold the necklace up for the customer to see it. Make the portable baby crib "look" easy to work. Lay the different pieces of the cookware set before the customer in an attractive, easy-to-see everything manner. Ask your salespeople to think like a customer, what would I like to see?

Message Adaptation. A knowledgeable salesperson should know about the products being sold. Message adaptation involves deciding what information is needed to sell a particular customer and how that information should be presented to that customer. Canned sales presentation do not allow for adaptation. The effective salesperson will make an effort to adjust the presentation to the customer. If the customer knows about gardens and lawns, the person selling a lawn service should adapt the sales presentation to the level of the customer's expertise. Don't bore the customer with known facts. It could lose a sale.

5. Handling Objections

Remember, if objections are present, progress is probably being made on the sale. Most salespeople are afraid of objections. Stress to all employees that objection are a natural part of the sales process. They do not mean that the sale is lost. In most cases, all that is required to overcome an objection is more sales on the part of the salesperson.

Common types of customer objections that are faced by a salesperson are:

Product: "That dress look out-of-date."

Store: "You never have the right kind of merchandise."

Service: "If I believe what I hear, I can't get good service from you."

Price: "It is just too expensive."

Salesperson: "Are you sure these shoes fit right?"

These and other objections can be met by the salesperson in several ways. Using the above product objection as an example, these methods include:

Yes-But. "Yes, it does look out-of-date, but it is the latest." This approach begins on a positive note by agreeing with the customer and then moves on to answer the objection.

Counter-question. "Why do you feel it's out-of-date?" By restating the objection, the customer may respond by saying, "No, I mean it just doesn't look right on me." or something of a similar nature. This approach tends to reduce the magnitude of the objection in the eyes of the customer.

Direct Response. "The dress you have on was first shown at the market this season. It is the latest thing." Although offensive to some, this approach may be necessary if the customer is not going to buy unless the untruth can be corrected. Tact is important when using this approach.

These four approached for handling objections are not meant to be all-inclusive. These and other approaches do point out, however, that objections should and can be answered by the salesperson. Unless objections are overcome to the satisfaction of the customer, it is questionable that the sale will be made.

6. Closing the Sale (Closing Skills)

In various ways, the salesperson can assist the customer by helping him or her to make the buying decision. Closing techniques that can aid in this effort include:

Offer a Service. "Let us deliver it to you this afternoon." A "yes" implies purchase.

Give a Choice. "Do you want the five-piece or eight-piece cooking set?" Either choice implies purchase. Note that "No" was not one of the choices.

Offer an Incentive. "If you buy now, you get 10% off the already low price." If you wait, you don't get the 10% discount.

Better Not Wait. "If you want this refrigerator, better get it now. It's the last one in stock." Note, it pays to be honest. If the customer buys and then comes by the store the next day and sees that the store did have another one, this closing technique may have made the sale but it could lose the customer.

7. Suggestion Sales Skills

The customer has made a purchase. Now what? Encourage your sales personnel to make a definite suggestion for a possible additional sale. For many businesses, sales can be increased by 25 percent through positive suggestion sales. Please note that statements such as: "Will there be something else?" or "Can I get you something else?" are not suggestion sales. They do not make a positive suggestion. When a customer buys a lamp, what about a light bulb to go in it? If a picture is purchased, what about the necessary hardware to hang it properly? If a suit is bought, what about a new blouse or shirt that goes well with the color? Where appropriate, the creative salesperson will actually get the suggested item and show it to the customer. Or if a person brings in a watch to be repaired, why not also clean it while it is taken apart? This type of initiative usually results in more sales. It should be emphasized that most customers like to receive a valid suggestion. In some cases, suggestions may even permit the customer to avoid another shopping trip to pick up that needed item that they had not thought about. Good suggestion sales makes sales and builds confidence in the firm's business.

8. Sales Follow-up

Although not apparent to many salespeople, follow-up is a part of every sale. The closing statement, "Thank you for shopping at (name of store)," is a form of sales follow-up if done with enthusiasm. Unfortunately, just making the statement in an automatic manner is about as effective as that other "worn out phrase," "May I help you?" If done correctly, however, it allows the customer to leave on a positive note, thereby increasing the chances of repeat business by the customer.

Follow-Up may also concern itself with checking on anything that was promised the customer after the sale. If delivery is supposed to take place on Friday, the salesperson will check to make sure the promise will be met and, if not, will notify the customer of the problem. Good sales follow-up will prevent the type of situation that occurs so often when the customer calls on Friday asking, "Where is the delivery truck?" A business with a reputation for sales follow-up is going to obtain additional business because of its concern after the sale. Sincere sales follow-up is good business. Imagine the impact that can be had on a customer when the carpet cleaning service telephones the customer 48 hours after cleaning to be sure that everything is satisfactory. Sales follow-up builds goodwill and repeat business.

Attribute of a creative salesperson

In addition to having personnel who understand and apply the creative selling process, an organization should try to have salespeople who possess certain attributes that can make them more effective in their jobs. These attributes, which can be grouped into mental and physical categories, merit further discussion.

Judgment

Common sense, maturity, intelligence - these and other terms are used interchangeably with judgment. A salesperson knows that it does not pay to argue with a customer. The salesperson also knows that the firm should never be "cut" in front of customers. These situations reflect the use of good judgment on the part of the employee. Please note that the term maturity is sometimes used in place of judgment but it is not necessarily a function of age. Many older people do not use good judgment while some young employees will have a high level of common sense.

Tact

If an employee has a keen sense of what to say and do, many problems can be overcome before they are created. Many employees give little thought to the impact of their actions. A child playing with toys in the toy store is told in a blunt manner to "quit playing with the toys and go find your mother." While all this is going on, the mother is standing behind the salesperson. Was a confrontation with the child necessary? No. Could it have been handled differently? Yes. How does the child and mother feel about the store? The feeling is not good. This salesperson lacked the ability to know what to do and say in order to maintain a good customer relations. Be tactful.

Attitude

A good salesperson will have a positive attitude toward customers, merchandise, services and the business. A good attitude means that an employee is willing to accept suggestions, to learn and to apply the steps in the creative selling process, and not to be afraid of work. A salesperson with a bad attitude can create unnecessary problems. A bad attitude is contagious. If any employee is otherwise competent, management should work with the employee to develop a positive attitude. Positive attitudes can result in sales.

Selected Physical Attributes

To be a success, the salesperson must physically belong in the firm's particular environment. Personal appearance and personal hygiene are important in the sales environment. In terms of personal appearance, a slim salesperson would be more appropriate than a larger person in a sales position at a health spa. Equally important in terms of personal appearance is a clothing salesman who wears last year's clothing. He will have difficulty in selling the latest fashions to his customers. Personal appearance does count in the sales equation.

As for personal hygiene - body odor, bad breath, dirty hair, soiled clothes, scuffed shoes, and unkept hands are all reasons why a sale may be lost. Obviously, be tactful when handling the problem of personal hygiene. An observant owner-manager should keep a watchful eye out for hygiene, problems among the staff and, when necessary, counsel the offending employee in private about improving his or her appearance. If you don't feel physical attributes are important, ask yourself if you would like to buy low-calorie health foods from an overweight salesperson with body odor. Sound funny? It isn't! Your customers will usually react unfavorably to this and similar inappropriate sales situations.

Word of Caution

Mental and physical attributes of salespersons are important. Management must continue to observe sales personnel in regard to the desired traits. Either mental or physical attributes of individuals may change over time relative to desired attributes. Management must be aware of this possibility and attempt to correct any deviations from desired norms before problems are created.

A business can greatly enhance its probability of success by stressing the creative selling process, giving special attention to the desired mental and physical attributes of a creative salesperson. Good creative selling can provide the competitive edge.

12. How to Prevent Shoplifting

Shoplifting and retail theft may not seem like major crime to the casual crook who pockets a ball-point pen here, a pocket calculator there. But to the small business fighting for survival, it's murder. There is a retail theft committed every five seconds in this country, These thefts cost each store owner $1200 a year. No store is immune.

A store operating at three percent profit on sales would have to sell $1,216.66 worth of merchandise a year to make up for the daily loss of a ten-cent candy bar. Just to cover a yearly loss of $1,000 in thefts, a retailer would have to sell each day over 900 candy bars, or 130 packs of cigarettes, or 380 cans of soup. Faced with such unreasonable selling volumes most small business people are forced instead to raise their prices and lower their ability to compete.

This Chapter contains practical advise on how to spot, deter, apprehend, and prosecute shoplifters.

Who's Robbing You Blind?

What does a shoplifter look like? Like you. Or like me. Shoplifters can be male or female, any race or color, as young as five or well into their 80's. Anyone who deliberately takes merchandise from a store without paying for it is a shoplifter, whether the theft is large or small, premeditated or impulsive.

Fortunately for business people, most shoplifters are amateurs rather than professionals. To the wary eye, they are not difficult to spot and, with the right kind of handling, they may never try petty thievery again. Here are the various types of shoplifters.

Juvenile offenders. Youngsters account for about 50 percent of all shoplifting and retail theft. They may steal on a dare or simply for kicks. Frequently they expect that store owners and courts will go easy on them because of their youth. They may enter stores in gangs in an attempt to intimidate management further. You simply cannot permit this kind of manipulation. youth is no excuse for crime, and the adult who lets it slips by is not doing the youngsters any favor. Shoplifting is usually the first type of theft attempted by juveniles, and it may lead to more serious crimes. Juvenile theft should be pursued and prosecuted through the proper legal channels.

Impulse shoplifters. Many "respectable" people fall into this category. They have not premeditated their thefts but a sudden chance (such as an unattended dressing room or a blind aisle in a supermarket) presents itself, and the shopper succumbs to temptation. the retailer can combat impulse shoplifting most effectively by simple prevention: building deterrents into the store layout and training employees to be aware of the problem and effective in dealing with it.

Alcoholics, vagrants and drug addicts. Abnormal physical need can drive people to theft, as well as to other crimes. These criminals are often clumsy or erratic in their behavior and may be easier than the other types of shoplifters to detect. The store owner should remember, however, that people under the influence of drugs or with an obsessive physical need may be violent. They may armed as well. It is best to leave the handling of such people to the police.

Kleptomaniacs. A driving psychological need can have similar effects. Kleptomaniacs are motivated by a compulsion to steal. They usually have little or no actual use for the items they steal and in many cases could well afford to pay for them. It is not up to the business person to make a psychological diagnosis. Shoplifting is shoplifting. It is no less simply because it is involuntary.

Professional. Since the professional shoplifter is in the business of theft, he or she is usually highly skilled and hard to spot. Professionals generally steal items which will quickly be resold to an established fence. They tend to concentrate on high-demand, easily-resold consumer goods such as televisions, stereos, and other small appliances. The pro, or "booster," may case a store or department well in advance of the actual theft. While professionals may be hard to prosecute (they may belong to underworld organizations which are very effective in raising bail and providing defense in court), they can be deterred from theft by effective layout and alert personnel.

How Do They Do It?

Shoplifters may work alone or in groups. while it's impossible to give an infallible rule of thumb, experience has shown that juveniles and professionals tend to work in groups, while the impulse shoplifter is a loner.

Working in a group, the shoplifter may use confederates to be concealed. One member of the gang may also start an argument with store personnel or among themselves, or even feign a fainting spell to draw attention, giving a cohort the opportunity to steal merchandise from another part of the store.

Shoplifters don't like crowds. They keep a sharp eye out for other customers or store personnel; quick, nervous glances may be a giveaway. They also tend to "shop" during hours when store staff is lighter than usual - during lunch hours, early morning, or just before closing.

Shoplifters also have their own arsenal of professional tools. Articles as innocent as bulky packages, pocket-books, baby carriages, knitting bags, shopping bags, umbrellas, newspapers and magazines can be used to carry stolen goods. Even an oversized arm sling can help the shoplifter conceal merchandise.

Specially-constructed devices such as coats or capes with hidden pockets and zippered hiding places are useful to the more experienced shoplifter. Some thieves use booster boxes (large boxes with a hinged end, top, or bottom). Booster boxes may be gift-wrapped to frustrate detection.

Unsupervised dressing rooms offer excellent opportunities for theft. Shoplifters may simply pile on layers of pilfered clothing, or they may exchange new items for the clothes they were wearing and return the originals to the rack.

Price tickets can be too often easily switched, particularly in grocery stores or drugstores where prices are written on gummed labels and often carelessly-stuck to the item.

How Can You Deter Shoplifters

Your time and money are better spent in preventing crime than prosecuting it. There are three major areas in which deterrence efforts pay off royally for the store owner.

1. Educate your employees. Train your sales help to be alert to the shoplifter's early warning signal. They should be on the lookout for customers carrying the concealment devices mentioned earlier in this Chapter. They should watch for shoppers walking with short or unnatural steps, tip-offs that the customers may be concealing items between their legs.

Clothing store employees should keep careful

count of the number of items carried into and out of dressing rooms.

Employees should be alert to groups of shoppers who enter the store together, then break up and go in different directions. A customer who attempts to monopolize a sales person's time may be covering for a confederate stealing elsewhere in the store.

Sales help should remember that ordinary customers want attention; shoplifters do not. When busy with one customer, the sales person should acknowledge waiting customers with polite remarks such as, "I'll be with you in a minute." This pleases legitimate customers, while making a shoplifter feel uneasy.

Sales people should watch for a customer who handles a lot of merchandise, but who takes an unusually long time to make a decision. They should watch for customers lingering in one area, loitering near stock rooms or other restricted areas or wandering aimlessly through the store. They should try to be alert to customers who consistently shop during hours when staff is low.

Cashiers should be trained to check the lower racks of shopping carts, to watch for switched price labels, to inspect containers such as garbage cans or tool boxes which could conceal stolen items.

Local police often conduct training seminars for store personnel. They can instruct your employees in spotting potential shoplifters, as well as in what to do when they observe a theft. Periodic review sessions, at least once every three months, will help keep employees aware.

You can help your employees help you. Schedule working hours to allow an adequate number of clerks to be on hand at all times. discourage "coffee-klatching" on the selling floor. A group of employees in one spot means inadequate coverage somewhere else.

2. Plan store layout with deterrence in mind. Maintain adequate lighting in all areas of the store. Keep protruding "wings" and end displays low, not more than two or three feet high. Set display cases in broken sequences. If possible, run them for short lengths with spaces in between.

Keep small items of high value (film, cigarettes, small appliances) behind a counter or in a locked case with sales clerk on duty. Keep displays neat; its easier to spot an item missing from an orderly array.

Attach noise alarms to unlocked exits. Close and block off unused checkout aisles. If you are involved in store design, plan to have entrances and exits in a common vestibule.

3. Use protective personnel and equipment. Protective devices may not be cheap, but shoplifting is costlier. You can get an idea of how much you can expect to lose to thieves by multiplying the number of shoplifters apprehended last year in your store by the average value of the stolen merchandise, then multiplying that figure by 50 weeks. The total is usually far greater than the cost of deterrence systems.

Some of the most widely-used devices are two-way mirrors, peep-hole, circuit television, convex wall mirrors, and detectives posing as customers, To be valuable, surveillance devices must be properly placed and monitored.

Uniformed guards are powerful visual deterrents to the shoplifter.

There are several ways to identify merchandise as having been legitimately paid for. One is to instruct cashiers to staple receipts to the outside of packages. Electronic tags may be attached to soft articles such as clothing. They can be removed only by a cashier with special shears, and they trigger an alarm if the shoplifter tries to carry the article from the store.

If you see electronic sensing devices, be sure cashiers are diligent in their use. If your employee forgets to remove the device and the customer is falsely accused, you could be liable.

Two-way radios make it easy to stay close to suspected shoplifters and to alert security personnel.

Ticket-switching can be discouraged through the use of tamper-proof gummed labels, hard-to-break plastic string, multiple price tickets concealed on items, or special staple or punch patterns on price tags

What About Apprehension, Arrest and Prosecution

While good deterrent systems will greatly reduce shoplifting, there are always people who are too dumb or too "smart" to be deterred. They'd try to steal the teeth out of a tiger's mouth if they thought the tiger wasn't looking.

These people could force you to the last line of defense for your store. Remember, to give your charges a chance of sticking, you must be able to:

See the person take or conceal merchandise,

Identify the merchandise as yours,

Testify that it was taken with the intent to steal,

Prove that the merchandise was not paid for.

If you are not able to meet all four criteria, you leave yourself open to the counter-charges of false arrest. False arrest need not mean police arrest; simply preventing a person from conducting normal activities can be deemed false arrest. Furthermore, any physical contact, even a light touch on the arm, may be considered unnecessary and used against you in court.

Check the laws in your state. Many states have passed shoplifting laws which deal with apprehension. Your lawyer or local police can advise you. Also, always consider your safety and that of your employees first and foremost.

In general, store personnel should never accuse customers of stealing, or should they try to apprehend suspected shoplifters. If they observe suspicious behavior or an apparent theft in progress, they should alert the store owner, manager, or store detective, or police.

It is wisest to apprehend shoplifters outside the store. You have a better case if you can show that the shoplifter left the store with stolen merchandise. Outside apprehension also eliminates unpleasant scenes which might disrupt normal store operation.

You may prefer to apprehend a shoplifter outside the store, if the merchandise involved is of considerable value or if you feel that the thief may be able to elude you outside the store premises.

In either case, avoid verbal accusation of the suspect. One recommended procedure is to identify yourself, then say, "I believe you have some merchandise which you have forgotten to pay for. Would you mind coming with me to straighten things out?"

When cornered, the first thing most shoplifter - impulse thieves or pros - will say is, I've never done this before." In general, this is all the more reason, if your evidence is sufficient, to call the police and proceed with prosecution. Failure to prosecute first offenders encourages them to try it again. Word also gets around that your store is an "easy hit."

Some organizations have control files on

shoplifter who have been caught. Your retail merchant's association can inform you about the services available in your area. You can check these files to see whether the person you catch has a prior record. a shoplifter who claims to be a first offender is likely to remain a " first offender "unless you get positive identification and file his or her name with the police and local retail merchant's association.

Naturally, each situation must be handled differently and your good judgment is required. You may wish to release elderly or senile shoplifters and not press charges where there's some indication that the person could honestly have forgotten to pay for the merchandise.

In most cases, however, prosecution is in order. It is essential if the shoplifter is violent, if he or she lacks proper identification and you suspect a prior record, if he or she appears to be under the influence of alcohol or other drugs, it the theft involves merchandise of great value, or if the shoplifter appears to be a professional.

Juvenile shoplifters require special handling. A strict, no-nonsense demeanor often makes a lasting impression on the young offender and may deter future theft, While many stores choose to contact the parents of young shoplifters rather than the police, remember that the juveniles account for half of all shoplifting that goes on in this country. The parents of troubled youngsters may be ineffective in handling the situation. Whom are you helping if you let the young shoplifter go to steal again?

13. Special Free Bonuses
(download links are provided)

a. Excel Financial Projections Creator - simply type in your business' details and assumptions and it will automatically produce a comprehensive set of financial projections for your specific business, including: Start-Up Expenses, Projected Balance Sheet, Projected Cash Flow Statement, Financial Ratios Analysis, Projected Profit and Loss Statement, Break Even Analysis, and many more.

Copy the following link to your browser and save the file to your PC:

http://www.bizmove.com/bp/projections.xlsx

b. Detailed guide that will walk you step by step and show you exactly how to effectively use the above Excel Financial Projections Creator.

Copy the following link to your browser and save the file to your PC:

http://www.bizmove.com/bp/projections-guide.doc

c. How to Improve Your Leadership and Management Skills (eBook) - Discover powerful strategies to motivate and inspire your people to bring out the best in them. Be the boss people want to give 200 percent for.

Copy the following link to your browser and save the file to your PC:

http://www.bizmove.com/bp/leadership.pdf

d. Small Business Management: Essential Ingredients for Success (eBook) - Learn effective business management tricks, secrets and shortcuts to make your business a success.

Copy the following link to your browser and save the file to your PC:

http://www.bizmove.com/bp/management.pdf

* * * *

Thank You for Reading My Book!

And I'm going to ask for a favor...

If you like this book... and if you'd be willing to spare just two or three minutes...would you be willing to share your review of the book on Amazon?

If you would, it would mean the absolute world to me!

Please leave me a supportive review by going to my Amazon book listing and tell me what you think in a review. This helps me get the book into as many hands as possible, helping others to start a successful business!

I really appreciate all your support.

- Meir Liraz